The Union

Cover picture: Queen Anne receiving the Treaty of Union in 1707.
Inside cover picture: The Parliament House in Edinburgh in 1707.
Title page picture: The Riding of the Scottish Parliament (the official Opening), 1690. The colour of the illustration was added later and may be incorrect.

First published in 1996 by Wayland (Publishers) Ltd,
61 Western Road, Hove, East Sussex BN3 1JD, England.

© Copyright 1996 Wayland (Publishers) Ltd.

British Library Cataloguing in Publication Data
Rose, Iain
   Union of 1707
   I. Title
   327.411042

ISBN 0 7502 1748 0

Editor: Katrina Maitland Smith
Consultant: Donald Gunn, Education Officer for BBC Education Scotland
Picture researcher: Elizabeth Miller
Concept design: Derek Lee
Book design and typesetting: Pardoe Blacker Limited
Printed and bound by B.P.C. Paulton Books, England

The right of Iain Rose to be identified as the Author of this work has been asserted in accordance with the Copyright, Designs and Patents Act 1988 Sections 77 and 78.

Picture acknowledgements
The publishers would like to thank the following for providing the illustrations for this book: AKG London 15 (top), 19, 24; e.t. archive (Christ's Hospital) 17 (top right); by permission of The British Library 21 (The Wafer's Map: 978 k.25); City of Bristol Museum and Art Gallery/Bridgeman Art Library, London 12 (left: BAG 13642); Mary Evans 13; Eye Ubiquitous/Paul Thompson 40; Glasgow Museums: Art Gallery & Museum, Kelvingrove 36-7; Historic Scotland (Edinburgh Castle) 11; reproduced by kind permission of the House of Commons cover (main picture); Impact 35 (left, Homer Sykes; right, Simon Shepheard); Mirror Syndication International 6; The National Trust (Ashdown House) 25; reproduced by kind permission of the Royal Bank of Scotland plc 20; reproduced by kind permission of the Royal College of Surgeons of Edinburgh 32 (right); Scotland in Focus/Jason Smalley 8; Scottish National Portrait Gallery cover (James VI and I), 10, 18, 27, 28; STB/Still Moving 26; © The Trustees of the National Museums of Scotland 1996 endpapers, title and contents pages, 15 (bottom), 23; Wayland 12 (right), 17 (bottom left, Angus Blackburn). The portrait on page 32 (left) is in a private collection.
Artwork is by: Peter Bull 17; Hardlines 7, 16, 21, 22; Richard Hook 29, 38; John Yates cover, imprint page.

# of 1707

Contents

Uniting Nations

In the evening of 28 October 1971, the British Parliament voted to join the EC. A crowd gathered outside the Houses of Parliament to hear the result of the vote.

In 1976, Great Britain joined the European Community, which is usually just called 'the EC' or 'the Common Market'.

The British had thought about becoming a member for many years before the British Government finally began talks with the EC about joining. These talks were called 'negotiations' and they lasted many months.

After everything was agreed, the British Parliament decided to hold a 'referendum'. This meant that everyone in Britain was allowed to vote either 'Yes' in favour of the agreement or 'No' against it.

The majority (58%) voted 'Yes' because they felt that becoming a member would benefit Britain. Some of those who voted 'Yes' hoped that it would become easier for Britain to buy and sell goods in Europe and that this trade would make Britain a richer country. Others thought that the EC would make another European war, like the First and Second World Wars, less likely.

The minority (42%) voted 'No'. Some did not believe that the EC would make Britain richer, while others did not like the British Parliament giving up some of its power to foreigners.

The argument about Britain and the EC is still going on.

In the past, before ordinary people were allowed to vote, they had no control over what happened to their country. The ruler of their country decided everything for them.

If the rulers of two countries married, their heir would inherit both countries and could combine them. Modern Spain was formed after King Ferdinand of Aragon married Queen Isabella of Castile and their son inherited both countries.

Rulers could also use force. Poland disappeared from the map of Europe for over one hundred years from 1772 because the rulers of Russia, Austria and Prussia decided to divide it up among themselves and the Poles were unable to stop them.

Today, most rulers no longer have that amount of power, and governments pay much more attention to the wishes of their people.

In modern democracies, every adult is allowed to vote and to choose his or her government. There are many things to argue about and discuss before governments can decide what to do.

In the past it was not like that.

This time-line shows how the Parliaments and Churches of Scotland and England became tangled in conflict after the Union of the Crowns in 1603. The Act of Union of 1707 settled most of these problems.

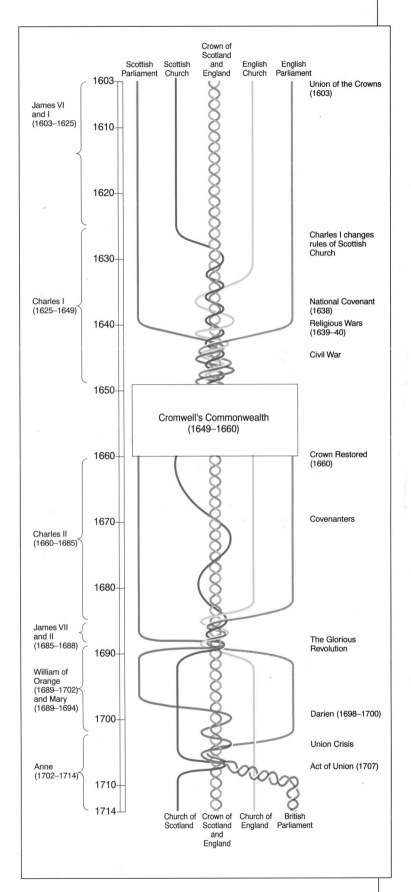

Scotland and England

For hundreds of years, Scotland and England were separate countries with their own monarchs and governments. They did not get on with each other because many of the kings of England tried to take over Scotland.

The most famous English ruler to attempt this was King Edward I. He was given the nickname 'The Hammer of the Scots' because of the way he kept attacking them. King Edward fought against King John Balliol, William Wallace and the Guardians of Scotland. His efforts were finally stopped by King Robert Bruce, who brought the Wars of Independence to an end in victory for the Scots.

To help protect their country against the kings of England, the Scots became friendly with France because it was England's main enemy. This friendship lasted for hundreds of years and was known as the 'Auld Alliance'. It did not always help the Scots.

When England went to war with France in 1513, King James IV of Scotland invaded England. His army was heavily defeated at Flodden. The King and many Scottish noblemen were killed. Scotland was then invaded by an English army, which destroyed everything it could before it went home.

The only survivor of Flodden from Selkirk brought back an English flag. The modern ceremony of 'Casting the Colours' remembers this.

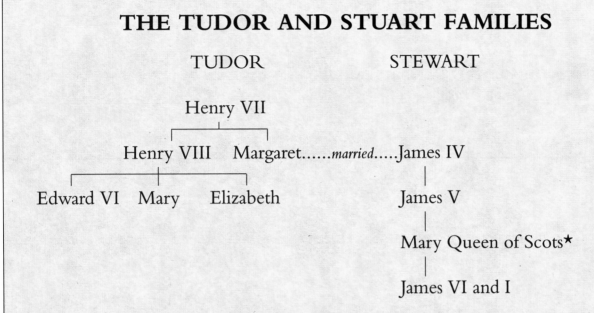

THE TUDOR AND STUART FAMILIES

TUDOR   STEWART

Henry VII

Henry VIII   Margaret......*married*.....James IV

Edward VI   Mary   Elizabeth   James V

Mary Queen of Scots★

James VI and I

★ Mary Queen of Scots used the French spelling of her surname, so it changed from Stewart to Stuart. She was the last ruler to be called King or Queen of Scots. After her rule, the title became King or Queen of Scotland.

Although there were many battles, and the Scots were often defeated, the English kings were never able to take over Scotland by force.

Sometimes, when the monarchs were on better terms, members of the two royal families married. In fact, this did little to stop the wars. King Alexander III was married to a sister of Edward, 'the Hammer of the Scots', but that did not stop Edward attacking Scotland to start the Wars of Independence.

James IV of Scotland was married to a daughter of Henry VII of England.

Henry VIII of England used both of these tactics, marriage and force, to try to take over Scotland. He wanted his young son, Edward, to marry the infant Mary Queen of Scots. She was the grand-daughter of King James IV and so was Henry's great-niece. When the Scots refused, Henry sent an army to Scotland. It caused a huge amount of damage in what the Scots called 'The Rough Wooing' but no marriage took place. Instead, the infant queen was sent to France where she married the king of France. So, Henry's efforts had brought his two enemies closer together.

None of Henry VIII's children, Edward VI, Mary Tudor or Elizabeth of England, had children, so the English Royal Family died out.

Elizabeth's closest relation was Mary Queen of Scots. After Mary's execution, Elizabeth's nearest relative was Mary's son, King James VI of Scotland. He became King James I of England when Elizabeth died in 1603. This was called the 'Union of the Crowns'.

A King with Two Kingdoms

King James VI of Scotland (1567–1625) and King James I of England (1603–1625).

After he became King of England, King James VI and I wanted to unite his two kingdoms into one country. He wanted to call it 'The United Kingdom of Great Britain'. He said that he felt like an animal with one head and two bodies. He thought that it would be better if the two countries were united.

The Scots and English did not want to do this. After hundreds of years of fighting they disliked each other too much. They would not even think about the idea!

Besides, there were many important ways in which the two countries were very different.

Language

The Scots and English spoke different languages. In the Highlands and Galloway, people spoke Gaelic. Lowland Scots spoke a language that they called Inglis. This was a northern form of English, which was very different from the English spoken further south. Many English noblemen complained that they could not understand King James VI and I!

Here is a poem about football, which was written, in Inglis, at the time of King James:

Brissit brawnis and brokin banis,
Stryf, discord and waistie wanis,
Cruikit in eild, syne halt withal -
Thir are the bewties of the fute-ball.

[Bruised bodies and broken bones
Strife, discord and broken homes.
Crooked in age; lame and all
These are the beauties of the football.]

Money

The two countries had their own money. Scotland was much poorer than England and Scots coins were not worth as much as English ones. In fact, an English pound (Sterling) was worth twelve pounds (Scots). The Scots did not see any need to change their coins.

Laws

The laws of Scotland and England were not the same. The Scots had borrowed ideas from Roman Law, which was used by many countries in Europe. England had not done so and, by 1603, there were big differences between the two systems. King James would find it very difficult to combine them.

Government

In both countries, the monarch chose men to help him to rule. These men were called 'Government Ministers'. They decided what to do at meetings of the 'Privy Council'.

The two Governments had different ways of doing things and nobody wanted these to change.

Trade

England was a rich country with much overseas trade around the world. Its Parliament did not want to share this with the Scots.

Parliament

Each country had a Parliament to make laws. Parliament also gave the Government permission to collect taxes from the people. Both Parliaments had been trying to gain power over their rulers by granting, or by refusing to grant, new taxes.

Whether they liked it or not, rulers had to pay attention to Parliament.

Religion

Scotland and England had different ideas about religion and how their Churches should be organized.

The Scottish Regalia were kept in Scotland after the Act of Union but they were hidden in a chest for one hundred years.

Religion

Until 1517, Christians in western Europe were united in one Church under the leadership of the Pope in Rome. The Pope decided what the Church would teach and who would have its most important jobs.

Then, a German monk called Martin Luther began to protest about some of the things the Church was doing. He wanted the Church to change and to reform itself. He started an argument which became so serious that the Church split up. This division is known as the 'Reformation'.

Martin Luther's supporters became known as 'Protestants'. People who continued to follow the Pope became known as 'Roman Catholics'.

Luther and his followers agreed about what they believed was wrong with the Roman Church. They could not, however, agree about what kind of Church they wanted in its place.

In some countries, the ruler took over the Church. Many royal families claimed that God had decided that their family would be rulers. This idea was called the 'Divine Right of Kings'.

During the Reformation these rulers decided to take over their countries' Churches. The rulers then chose the archbishops and bishops, so the Church always agreed with whatever they wanted.

This is what happened in England when Henry VIII became a Protestant. In Scotland, things were very different.

John Knox, who made Scotland a Protestant country.

Martin Luther, the German Reformer.

John Knox led the Scottish Reformation. He did not believe that rulers should have any power over God's Church. This was because he believed everyone was equal in God's eyes. He wanted the members of the Church to run it for themselves.

This meant that the Church was free to complain about rulers who did not live good, religious lives. John Knox did not think twice about giving his ruler, Mary Queen of Scots, a telling off when he thought she deserved it. This made Mary extremely angry, but there was nothing she could do to stop him.

Her son, King James VI and I, was determined to take control of the Scottish Church.

Knox had allowed the people to elect their own Church ministers. He had also decided that there should be superintendents who would check up on these ministers. King James wanted to choose the superintendents himself. He planned to use them like bishops, to help him control the Church.

This was not easy because, after Knox died, the Presbyterian Andrew Melville became the most powerful man in the Church. Melville did not want any royal control of the Church. He called King James 'God's silly vassal' (God's simple servant) and said that, in the Church of Scotland, 'James VI was not a king, nor a lord, nor a head, but a member' – just like everyone else.

King James was furious. He was determined to have bishops. He took his

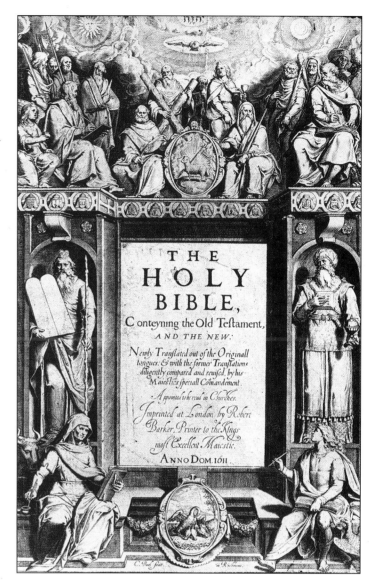

King James had the Bible translated from Latin into English. This translation was used for 350 years. The title page pictured above is from the 1611 edition.

time, used all his cunning and, at last, he got what he wanted. The Scottish Church became 'episcopal'. This means 'having bishops' and it comes from the Latin word, *episcopus*, meaning bishop.

The Presbyterians were not happy about this change. There was going to be more trouble.

Parliament and Religion

The Scottish Parliament never represented the people of Scotland. In fact, it represented only four groups:

The Bishops – chosen by the king;

The Lords of Parliament – 160 noblemen with titles like Duke, Earl, or Lord;

The Lairds – important landowners. The lairds from each county elected two lairds as Members of Parliament (MPs) for their county;

The Royal Burghs – 66 special towns. Each sent an MP to Parliament.

These four groups met together in Parliament. Their meetings could last for a long time, which made them very expensive. So, the Scots Parliament usually just elected a smaller 'Committee of the Articles' to do its work.

After he went to England, King James VI and I persuaded the Scots Parliament to change the rules for electing this committee. The bishops chose eight lords and the lords chose eight bishops. These 16 men chose eight lairds and eight townsfolk. James added eight members of his government. The full Committee of the Articles had 40 members.

But James had chosen the bishops and they always obeyed him. He told them which lords to choose. These bishops and lords then chose the lairds and townsfolk James wanted.

King James controlled the whole Committee of the Articles.

King James was pleased with the control he had over Scotland. He boasted, 'Here I sit and govern with my pen, I write and

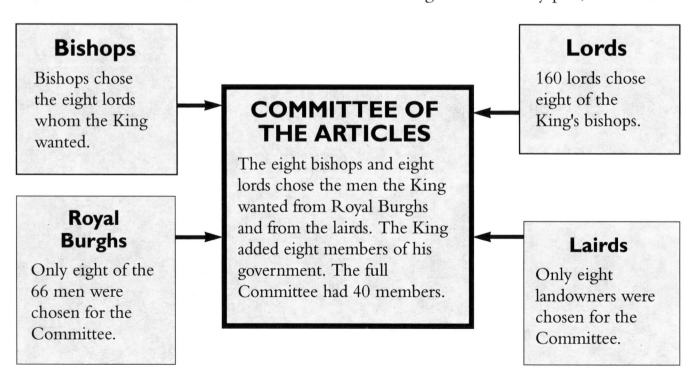

Bishops

Bishops chose the eight lords whom the King wanted.

Royal Burghs

Only eight of the 66 men were chosen for the Committee.

COMMITTEE OF THE ARTICLES

The eight bishops and eight lords chose the men the King wanted from Royal Burghs and from the lairds. The King added eight members of his government. The full Committee had 40 members.

Lords

160 lords chose eight of the King's bishops.

Lairds

Only eight landowners were chosen for the Committee.

it is done.' However, he was always very careful about what he did.

His son, King Charles I, was not so clever. He wanted to make the Scottish Church more like the Church of England. He wanted the Scottish Church to emphasize the Divine Right of Kings. To do this, he needed to change the religious ideas of the Scots.

Charles I used his power over the bishops to make the changes he wanted. He ignored the complaints and warnings from Scotland. There were riots when his new Prayer Book was first used in Scotland in July 1637.

In Edinburgh, the trouble became so serious that the Scottish Privy Council asked the rioters to meet together and write down their complaints in detail.

In February 1638, the protesters wrote a petition, which they called the National Covenant. Copies of it were sent all over Scotland and people rushed to sign it – some even wrote using their own blood. It seemed as if the whole country was united against the King.

King Charles decided to make the Scots obey him. He gathered an army and marched on Scotland. The Scots gathered an army to fight against their King. It looked as if there was going to be a civil war.

Left: King Charles I (1625–1649). When he tried to change Scotland's religion, many Scots signed the National Covenant (below) to complain.

Religious Wars

The Scots had all agreed to fight King Charles I for religious reasons. Soon, however, they began to quarrel about how much power King Charles ought to share with his Parliaments. This argument was also an important reason for the civil war starting in England at this time.

Fighting began in Scotland when the Marquis of Montrose gathered an army of Highlanders and Irishmen to fight for King Charles. Montrose felt that some Scottish noblemen, like the Marquis of Argyll, were fighting the King just to take power for themselves.

Although he won some great victories, Montrose was finally defeated and forced to leave the country.

King Charles lost the civil war. Oliver Cromwell, who led the English Parliament's army, took the King prisoner. Charles was put on trial, accused of making war against his subjects. He was found guilty and was beheaded in January 1649.

Cromwell then announced that, because England did not have a king, it was no longer a 'kingdom'. He called England a 'Commonwealth' and made himself its 'Protector'.

The Scots were horrified. They decided to fight for King Charles' son, Charles II, if he would agree to support the National Covenant and the Presbyterian Church.

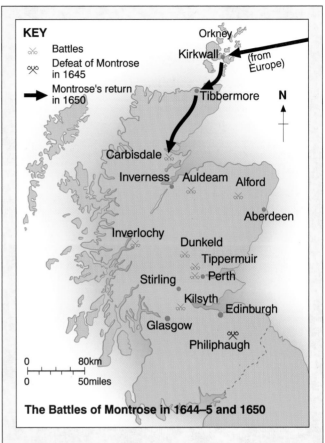

The Battles of Montrose in 1644–5 and 1650

Montrose's enemies had bigger armies than him but he won all the battles until he was surprised at Philiphaugh. After he was defeated he fled to Europe.

Montrose returned in 1650 to fight for Charles II but he was captured and executed.

This verse by Montrose tells what he thought about fighting:

He either fears his fate too much,
Or his deserts are small,
That puts it not unto the Touch
To win or lose it all.

Cromwell defeated the Scots army at Dunbar and again at Worcester. In 1652, he made Scotland part of the Commonwealth. He allowed the Scots to send 30 Members of Parliament to Westminster in London.

The Scots did not like the loss of their independence. On the other hand, they were allowed to trade with England's colonies in America because they were united with England. Some Scots became very rich.

After Cromwell's death, his Commonwealth did not last long. In 1660, Charles II took control of Scotland and England. He decided to cancel every change that had happened in Scotland after 1633. The Scots were delighted to become a separate kingdom again.

There were some disadvantages. The Scots were not allowed to trade with England's colonies any more. The Committee of the Articles took over their Parliament and bishops returned to the Church of Scotland.

Some Presbyterians felt that it was more important to obey their God than their king. They believed in the ideas of the National Covenant of 1638, so they were called 'Covenanters'. A few of them were so certain that they were right and the King was wrong that they even declared war on King Charles II. For doing this, they were hunted down and killed.

King Charles wanted to make sure that everyone in Scotland agreed that he was in charge of their Church. This made many Scots suspicious of him.

King Charles II (1660–1685) punished Covenanters for supporting the National Covenant of 1638.

This monument shows where many Covenanters were executed.

The Glorious Revolution

When King Charles II died in 1685, his brother became King James VII of Scotland and II of England. King James was a Roman Catholic and wanted to change the laws against his Church. His Parliaments would not do this, so he changed the laws himself. He also gave Roman Catholics important jobs in his Government.

This made King James very unpopular. Some people were so upset that they went to Holland, where King James' daughter, Mary, and her husband, William of Orange, lived. People hoped that William and Mary would be their next rulers, because they were Protestants and supported Parliament.

King James had other ideas. He remarried and, in 1688, he had a son who would be brought up as a Catholic. By the Law of Succession his son would become the next ruler.

Many nobles wrote secretly to William and Mary, inviting them to become rulers instead of King James. When William of Orange landed at Torbay in England towards the end of 1688, King James fled to France. There he, and later his son, plotted a return to Britain. Their supporters were known as 'Jacobites' – the name comes from *Jacobus*, the Latin word for James.

Many Scots were still prepared to obey King James VII and II if he promised to be a better ruler in future. However,

King James VII and II (1685–88) was unpopular because of his religion.

William and Mary had Scottish supporters among the Presbyterians.

Both James and William wrote to the Scottish Parliament. William was very polite and said he would support Parliament and the Protestants. James' letter was filled with threats and said

William of Orange became King William II of Scotland and William III of England.

nothing about religion. More people then turned against James.

Finally, in 1689, the Scottish Parliament decided that James was no longer king because he had been such a bad ruler. It said that he had 'forfeited' the crown. In the 'Claim of Right', Parliament laid down new rules, which William and Mary had to accept before Parliament would let them rule.

After that, Parliament went on to tackle the problem of Scotland's Church.

The bishops said that only God could decide who their ruler should be. They supported King James and even called

him 'the darling of the heavens'. They said that Parliament could not make William and Mary rulers.

So, Parliament decided to abolish bishops and to return to the Presbyterian system. In future, the members of each church would elect their own minister. Those ministers who continued to support bishops were driven out of their churches.

Parliament also abolished the Committee of the Articles. It felt that this Committee had given King James far too much power. After this, the Scottish Parliament could discuss whatever it wanted. This made it much more difficult for the ruler to control Scotland and, within a few years, it was causing problems for King William.

THE CLAIM OF RIGHT

The crown had been taken away from King James VII and II.

No Roman Catholic could be ruler.

Rulers could not change laws by themselves.

Only Parliament could allow taxes.

Parliament should meet more often.

Torture was to be abolished for ordinary crimes.

There should be no bishops in Scotland.

The Company of Scotland

The Scottish Parliament knew that Scotland needed to trade with other countries if it was to become a wealthy nation.

Many people felt that Scotland had become poorer after the Union of the Crowns in 1603. They felt that the king, far away in London, did not pay enough attention to Scotland. Besides, whenever England went to war, Scotland had to go to war as well. Scottish trade was badly affected by these wars but, when peace was made, Scotland was given nothing to make up for its losses.

The Scots knew that England had grown rich by trading overseas, especially with colonies where the English had settled. These colonies were an English monopoly: only the English were allowed to trade with them. Scottish traders were banned from these colonies.

The Scots also knew that huge amounts of money could be earned through trade with Africa and the Indies. The 'East India Company' was the only English company allowed to trade in India. This monopoly made it very rich and powerful. The Scots began to think about setting up a Scottish Trading Company to do the same thing.

The Coat of Arms of The Company of Scotland showed that it wanted to earn money by carrying goods all over the world. The St. Andrew's Cross has a ship, an elephant, a camel and a llama around it. The rising sun promised a good future.

William Paterson had the idea of setting up 'The Company of Scotland Trading to Africa and the Indies'. His idea for setting up the Bank of England had already been a success, and Paterson had friends with money in both Scotland and England. His plan for The Company of Scotland was to give it the Scottish monopoly in trade with Africa and the Indies.

Paterson knew that the Scots did not have enough money to do this by themselves. He wanted half of the money to come from English merchants who wished to trade with the Indies. This plan upset the East India Company, which saw the Company of Scotland as a powerful rival. The East India Company created such a fuss in the English Parliament that no Englishmen dared to join the Company of Scotland.

King William was in a difficult position because the English and Scottish Parliaments wanted different things. He could not please both.

The Scottish Parliament was determined to set up the Company of Scotland. It decided to ask friends in Holland and the German city of Hamburg to join the Company. When the East India Company complained to King William, he wrote to these people warning them not to give the Scots any money.

The angry Scots decided to raise all the money by themselves. This was not easy because Scotland was not rich. People made a terrific effort. Some gave the Company all the money they had. Others even borrowed money to help it. Soon the Company had all the money it wanted but it still had to decide where to set up its colony.

William Paterson suggested Darien, on central America's narrow Isthmus of Panama between the Atlantic and Pacific Oceans.

This old map shows that Darien lay between the Atlantic Ocean to the north and Pacific Ocean to the south.

William Paterson called Darien, 'The door of the seas and the key of the Universe.' He wrote, 'The time and expense of sailing from China will be reduced by more than half. Trade will increase trade and money will make money.'

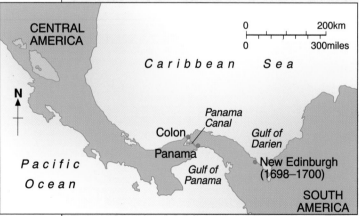

Today, ships use the Panama Canal to avoid the long and dangerous journey around South America.

The Darien Disaster and the 'Ill Years'

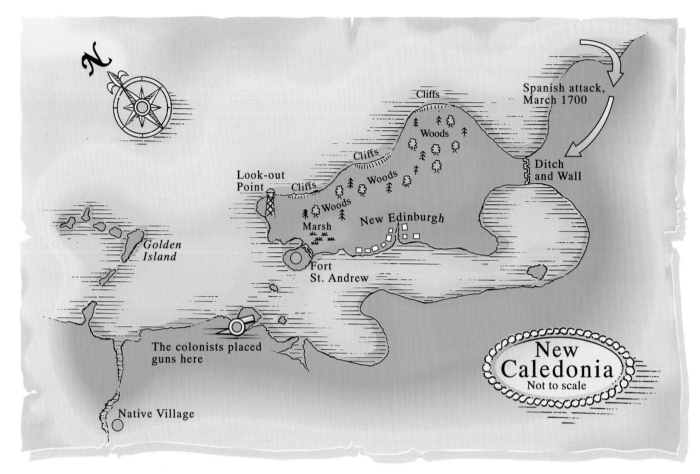

This map shows how the Scots colonists saw their 'New Caledonia', and how they tried to protect it from attack.

Paterson's great idea of a Scottish colony in South America was a disaster. Most of the people who went there died and the Company of Scotland lost nearly all its money.

Setting sail in July 1698, it took four months for the first group of colonists to reach Darien. During the journey, their ships ran short of food and water. When they arrived in Darien, most colonists were too weak and ill to work. They had also started to quarrel among themselves.

They called their colony New Caledonia and began to build Fort Saint Andrew and the town of New Edinburgh. However, New Caledonia was not a healthy area, and many of the colonists caught fevers and died.

The survivors continued to argue among themselves because they were very short of food and they had heard nothing from Scotland.

They had become friendly with the native peoples, but these had told the

Spanish about New Caledonia. The Spanish had first settled in Darien over a hundred years earlier. They said that Darien was part of the Spanish Empire and they did not want the Scots to settle there.

The Spanish complained to King William about his Scottish subjects trying to settle on their land.

King William could not tell the Scots to leave Darien, but he did not want to upset the Spanish. To please them, and the East India Company, he ordered that nobody was to help the Scots colonists.

By themselves, the New Caledonians could not survive and, in June 1699, they abandoned Darien and sailed back to Scotland.

The Company of Scotland knew nothing about this when, in September 1699, it sent more colonists to Darien. They arrived three months later and were astonished to find New Caledonia deserted. They began to rebuild the town and the fort but they, too, suffered terribly from fevers and shortages. Then, the Spanish came to attack them.

Although the Scots defeated the Spanish soldiers, the Spanish navy managed to blockade Caledonia Bay. Nothing could sail in or out of the harbour. In the spring of 1700, the Scots agreed to abandon their colony for good.

Only one of their ships made it back to Scotland. The others were either wrecked or abandoned on the way.

The failure of Darien was a disaster for Scotland because a huge amount of money had been lost. Many Scots lost their savings. Those who had borrowed money to help the Company of Scotland were made to sell everything to pay off their debts. Nearly everyone blamed King William because he had not supported their efforts.

The Darien Disaster could not have happened at a worse time for the Scots. For five years after 1695, the harvests in Scotland were very poor. Many people starved to death because there was no food. There were stories that, in some places, as much as half of the population died during the 'Ill Years'.

Farmers could not afford to pay their rents, so even the rich land-owners found them-selves short of money. This made the loss of money in Darien even more serious.

The lock inside the lid of the Company of Scotland's money chest.

The Succession Crisis

King William became very unpopular in Scotland. The Jacobites had never wanted him and blamed him for the Glencoe Massacre in which his soldiers murdered 38 Jacobite MacDonalds. This scandal also upset many people who were not Jacobite.

The Scottish Presbyterians were annoyed when King William gave Episcopalians permission to have their own churches in Scotland. The Presbyterians were worried that King William might bring back bishops.

Some people even said that the 'Ill Years' were King William's fault. Everyone blamed him for the Darien Disaster.

King William realized that it was impossible to please both the Scots and the English if their Parliaments disagreed. He suggested that the two should unite to make a single 'British' Parliament.

This idea was unpopular in both countries and King William died before he had time to do anything about it. The two Parliaments then began a huge argument with each other about 'The Succession' – who were to be the future rulers of Scotland and England?

King William and Queen Mary had no children. Their heir was Mary's sister, Anne, who became Queen when King William died in 1702. All of Anne's sixteen children had died and she had no obvious heir. Her Parliaments would have to decide who their next ruler would be.

Queen Anne (1702–1714) was the last of the Stuart family to rule Scotland and England.

The Scots and English Parliaments had already agreed that their ruler had to be a Protestant. This meant that they would not accept Anne's step-brother, James, whom the Jacobites supported.

In the Act of Succession of 1701, the English Parliament had decided that, after Queen Anne died, the English throne would go to her second cousin, Sophia. Sophia was married to a German ruler, called the 'Elector of Hanover', so Parliament called this plan 'The Hanoverian Succession'.

Then the English Parliament made a serious mistake. It decided that its Act of Succession would be the law for Scotland. This annoyed the Scots because the English Parliament had no right to make laws for Scotland.

The Scots became angry when England went to war with France in 1702. The Scots did not want a war because it would harm their trade. To please the Queen, her Scottish Ministers decided that Scotland should join in the fighting. The Scottish Parliament resented the fact that nobody had asked what it wanted.

Queen Anne decided that, just like King William, she wanted her two Parliaments to unite. Some angry Scots had very different ideas. Rather than have a Union of Parliaments, they wanted to end the Union of Crowns.

Sophia, a grand-daughter of King James VI and I, married the Elector of Hanover. Their son became King George I of Britain.

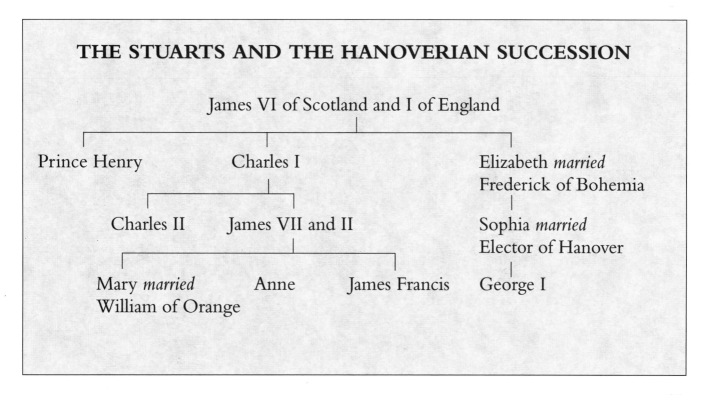

THE STUARTS AND THE HANOVERIAN SUCCESSION

James VI of Scotland and I of England

Prince Henry   Charles I   Elizabeth *married* Frederick of Bohemia

Charles II   James VII and II   Sophia *married* Elector of Hanover

Mary *married* William of Orange   Anne   James Francis   George I

The Bad-Tempered Parliament

The Scottish Parliament met at Parliament Hall in Edinburgh until the Act of Union. Today, Parliament Hall is known as Advocates Hall. (An advocate is a lawyer.)

Many Scots were angry about the way Scotland had been governed. One of Queen Anne's Scottish Ministers warned her about '...the bad temper this nation has been in for some years.'

Scottish MPs planned to make a big fuss about the Succession in the hope that they could force the Government to make changes. Their problem was that they did not agree about which changes they wanted.

The Jacobites did not want the Hanoverian Succession. They wanted the Roman Catholic son of King James VII and II to be their next king. The Jacobites called him King James VIII.

Andrew Fletcher of Saltoun said that Scotland was badly governed because its ruler was too far away in London. He said that Scotland was 'totally neglected, like a farm run by servants and not under the eye of its owner.' He wanted to give more power to the Scottish Parliament.

Others, like the Duke of Hamilton, just blamed everything on the Queen's Ministers. They hoped that, if they caused enough trouble for the Queen, she would sack her Ministers and give them jobs instead.

In fact, the Queen had very few supporters in the Scottish Parliament.

When the Scottish Parliament discussed the Succession, it agreed with the English Parliament that its next ruler would have to be a Protestant member of the Stuart Royal Family. Then, in the 'Act of Security', it showed its bad temper. It decided that it would not choose the same ruler as England unless Scots were allowed to trade with England's colonies.

The English were horrified. They did not want to let the Scots trade with their colonies, but they did not want Scotland to have a separate ruler again. They were worried that, if this happened, there would be more wars between England and Scotland.

The Scots, too, had difficulties with the Act of Security. In the first place, the Hanoverians were the only Protestant members of the Stuart Royal Family. There was nobody else to be their ruler. The Duke of Hamilton said that he was a distant relation of the Royal Family, but nobody thought that he was really 'royal' enough to become king.

Secondly, the Act of Security said nothing about how Scotland would be governed if the English agreed to give them trade privileges and they continued to share a ruler.

Their ruler would still have two Parliaments, which could still fall out with each other.

The Duke of Hamilton

The Duke of Hamilton was an important leader in the Scottish Parliament. He wanted money and power but he was never sure about what power he wanted and whose money he should take.

He knew that, if the Scots did not accept the Hanoverian Succession, he was Queen Anne's closest Protestant relation. He thought he could be King of Scots. He also knew that, if he tried to become king and failed, he would be in serious trouble with Queen Anne and the Hanoverians.

He always needed money. He was once compared to a 'room for rent' – whoever offered him most money would buy his support! He even spoke to Jacobite spies.

Bad Feelings

Fletcher of Saltoun complained loudest against 'the power of English Ministers over this nation.'

The Scottish Parliament had other ways to show how annoyed it was. It refused to give the Government any money, so nobody could be paid!

The French war was not popular in Scotland because it had a bad effect on Scotland's trade with Europe. The Scots were angry because the Queen's Government had started the war without asking their Parliament. So, in the 'Wine Act', the Scottish Parliament gave Scots permission to trade with France again, even though the two countries were at war.

In the 'Act Anent [about] War and Peace' it decided that, in future, the Government could not start, or finish, a war without the Scottish Parliament's permission.

Fletcher of Saltoun then wanted the Scottish Parliament to take over almost all of the ruler's power. He said, 'I don't want to reduce the power of the King of Scotland, but the power of English Ministers over this nation.'

By this time, the English Parliament was very worried about what was happening in Scotland. In the 'Aliens Act' it threatened to stop all of Scotland's trade with England unless the Scots cancelled their Act of Security and agreed to either a Union of Parliaments or the Hanoverian Succession.

A trade ban would have ruined Scotland and caused trouble in England because England needed Scottish goods. In fact, the Aliens Act may just have been a threat. Some Englishmen also began to talk about soldiers being moved to the Scottish border, but that may just have been another threat.

THE WORCESTER INCIDENT

In 1704, the Company of Scotland's last ship was taken over by English taxmen to please the East India Company.

The Company of Scotland then took over an English ship, the *Worcester*. They planned to sell it and its cargo. This was popular because the Scots still blamed the English for the Darien Disaster.

The Scots also suspected that Captain Green of the *Worcester* knew something about the earlier disappearance of another of the Company of Scotland's ships, the *Speedy Return*. They accused Captain Green and his crew of being pirates.

There was little to prove this, but the Captain and two of his sailors were found guilty and sentenced to death.

The English asked Queen Anne to pardon Green and his crew. This would have set them free. The Queen thought that this would make the Scots even angrier. She wanted her Scottish Ministers to grant the pardon instead.

The Ministers had a difficult problem. If they freed Green and his crew, they would please the Queen but anger the Scots. If they allowed the men to hang, they would anger the Queen but please the Scots.

The Edinburgh mob decided the matter. A huge number of people demonstrated against a pardon. They sounded so ferocious that the Ministers did not dare to set Captain Green and his sailors free. The mob followed the condemned men all the way from Edinburgh Castle to Leith Links, where they were hanged.

Within two weeks, the Scots realized that they had made a terrible mistake. They discovered that Green and his crew had nothing to do with the disappearance of the *Speedy Return*.

Captain Green being led to his execution on Leith Links. He expected to be pardoned; but he wasn't.

Preparing for a Union

The Duke of Argyll wanted the Scots to agree to the Hanoverian Succession and an Act of Union.

In 1705, Queen Anne gave the Duke of Argyll control over her Government in Scotland. He was a soldier and believed that people had to obey orders. He also wanted money and titles for himself and his family.

In a letter he wrote, 'I'm surprised that the Government uses me like a servant, without offering me a reward. There should be an offer of a reward.'

Argyll was determined to earn his reward by persuading the Scots to agree to a Treaty of Union and to the Hanoverian Succession. To do this, Argyll offered privileges to win votes.

Here are some of the things he did.

Jobs and Titles

There were many government jobs, which paid good salaries. Argyll told everyone with a government job to vote for the Government or be sacked!

He also promised people new jobs if they obeyed him. The Earl of Rosebery wanted to be 'Chamberlain of Fife' and to be paid £300 a year. This would be worth more than £30,000 today! Rosebery did what he was told and, in time, he was given the job.

The Earl of Glasgow was awarded the Register's Office and was paid £1,200 a year for his work in winning support for the Union.

Friends and relations of people in Parliament were also offered jobs.

Some people wanted to become noble and to have a title. The Queen would give people new noble titles like Lord, Viscount, Earl, Marquis or Duke if they supported Argyll.

Some noblemen wanted to be promoted to a more important title than the one they already had. The Earl of Roxburghe wanted to become a Duke, so he did what Argyll said.

Money

Nowadays, offering people money to vote for you is against the law. In the past, it was quite common, but people kept quiet about it.

Bribes

The Government used £20,000 to bribe people. This is what some of the people received:

Duke of Queensberry	£12,000
Earl of Marchmont	£1,000
Campbell of Cessnock	£50
Lord Banff	£11.10p

Pensions

Pensioners were paid money by the Government every year for as long as they lived.

William Seton of Pitmedden was paid £100 a year for writing newspaper articles in favour of the Union.

The Earl of Glencairn was offered a pension. He lost it because he did not do what the Government wanted.

Debts

People who worked for the Government expected to be paid. Argyll told people who voted against the Government that they would have to wait years and years for their money. Most people needed the money, so they supported the Union.

Spies and Threats

The Government in London sent the writer, Daniel Defoe, to Scotland as a spy. His job was:

- to find out about groups against the Union and to stop them;

- to persuade people to support the Union;

- to answer any arguments made against the Union.

Later, Defoe wrote, 'Nobody suspects that I am writing to England. I talk to everybody and at the end of every conversation I say that the Union is essential.'

He even boasted, 'I have spies everywhere.'

In another letter he wrote, 'Money can do anything here.'

By using spies, Argyll found out that many Scottish noblemen, like the Duke of Hamilton, had been in contact with the Jacobites.

This was against the law and these noblemen could be jailed or even executed. Argyll could threaten to arrest these men unless they did what he wanted.

In these ways Argyll and his helpers, the Duke of Queensberry and the Earl of Seafield, won support for the Government in Parliament.

In August 1705, Parliament began to discuss a Treaty of Union with England.

Deciding on the Union

The Duke of Queensberry (left) was a very powerful Scottish nobleman who wanted a Union with England. He was one of the Scottish Commissioners, as was the Earl of Seafield (right).

Queen Anne decided that a few men from each country would meet to draw up a plan for a Union. These men were called 'Commissioners'. Both Parliaments would have to agree with the plan before any Union could happen.

The Commissioners had a very important job. If they worked together, they could make a Union easy. If they fell out, they could stop a Union happening. That was why the Government and its opponents argued about who the Commissioners should be.

The Government wanted the Queen to choose them because she would choose men who wanted a Union.

Opponents of a Union wanted Parliament to choose the Commissioners. They wanted it to choose men to wreck the Government's plans.

The Jacobites were against any Union. They thought a Union would make it difficult to have a Jacobite ruler. Fletcher of Saltoun and his friends were against it because they did not think that it would make the government of Scotland better.

The debate about choosing Commissioners began on 24 August 1706. The discussion was still going on a week later. Both sides were taking their time before having a vote.

The leading opponent of a Union was the Duke of Hamilton. On 1 September, he told his friends that there would be no vote about Commissioners on that day. The talking went on late into the night. Many of the opposition had left Parliament when, suddenly, the Duke of Hamilton stood up and suggested that the Queen should choose Commissioners. He had changed sides!

Fifteen of the opposition then ran out of the Parliament building to warn their friends about what had happened. While they were away, the Government called a vote about who would choose Commissioners and won by four votes. The Queen was to choose them.

In February 1706, the Queen announced the list of Commissioners. Thirty of the 31 Scottish Commissioners were in favour of a Union. The English Commissioners also wanted it, so there were hardly any arguments.

The two groups never met. They gathered in separate rooms and wrote notes to each other. This was to avoid any misunderstandings. Their meetings were secret. They did not want anyone to find out anything until the whole plan was prepared.

Eventually, after several months of work, the Commissioners produced their plan, which was called 'The Articles of Union'.

Why did Hamilton do it?

Nobody knows why Hamilton changed sides so suddenly. There are many suggestions.

Firstly, Hamilton needed money. He might have been bribed.

Secondly, Argyll might have threatened to arrest Hamilton for speaking to the Jacobites.

Thirdly, Hamilton's wife was English. She had a huge amount of land in England, and Hamilton was worried about what might happen if the two countries fell out.

Fourthly, Argyll may have offered Hamilton a job as one of the Commissioners. (In fact, Hamilton was not chosen for the job.)

Andrew Fletcher

Andrew Fletcher of Saltoun was always against a Union.

This description of him was written in 1705: 'A short, thin man, full of fire and with a stern, sour look. He is a gentleman with a lot of learning. He is as brave as the sword he wears and bold as a lion. He would lose his life gladly to serve his country and would not do a bad thing to save it.'

The Articles of Union

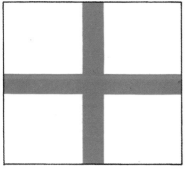

St. George's Cross
(England)

St. Andrew's Cross
(Scotland)

First Union Flag

The Articles of Union said that:

- the two kingdoms of Scotland and England were to become the United Kingdom of Great Britain;

- they agreed to the Hanoverian Succession;

- the Scottish and English flags would be joined to form the Union Flag.

The St. Andrew's Cross of Scotland and the St. George's Cross of England were put together to produce a new flag for the Union. Today's Union flag, or Union Jack, was created when the Irish St. Patrick's Cross was added when Ireland joined the Union in 1800.

Parliament

Compared with the English Parliament, the Scottish Parliament was far too big. England had five times as many people as Scotland and was far richer. Its Parliament had 180 lords and 513 people in the House of Commons. The Scots Parliament had 160 lords and 155 lairds and townspeople.

After much discussion, it was decided that the Scottish lords would elect 16 lords to go to the new British House of Lords. After the Union, all new noble titles would be British. The new British nobles would all be allowed to go to the House of Lords in London. Many Scottish lords then tried to obtain new British titles for themselves; the Duke of Queensberry became Lord Dover.

Scotland was allowed only 45 Members in the British House of Commons. Scottish landowners elected 30 Members of Parliament and the Royal Burghs elected 15. The Scots did not think this was fair, but they were forced to agree to it.

The Law

The Law and system of Courts in Scotland were not changed. The laws of Scotland and England are still different from each other – as are the uniforms worn by the Scottish police (left) and English police (right).

The Equivalent

The English Government had borrowed money from abroad which meant that England had a big 'national debt'. The English paid more taxes than the Scots.

Scotland didn't have a national debt or many taxes. When the two countries united, the Scots would have to pay more taxes to pay for England's national debt. This was not fair, so Scotland was given money when the Union happened. This was called the 'Equivalent'.
The Equivalent was in three parts:

- the first part paid the bills of the Scottish Government – like wages;

- the second part was paid to people who had given money to the Company of Scotland. They received all their money back and an extra 5% (£5 for every £100);

- the final part was used to help Scottish industry.

This money persuaded some Scots that the Union would be a good idea. But they had to wait years for it.

Free Trade

Money and Measures

Since they would be one country, the Scots could trade with all of England's colonies. This was why some Scots, like the Earl of Cromartie, wanted a Union.

'Free Trade' also meant that Englishmen could trade with Scotland. Many Scottish towns were worried that they would be ruined if people bought cheap things made in England rather than in Scotland.

To make it easier for the two countries to trade, the Commissioners decided that there would be one system of money, weights and measures.

Scottish money would be abolished and replaced by the English 'Pound Sterling'. The 'Scots Pound' was worth less than the 'Pound Sterling'. People got £1(Sterling) for every £12(Scots).

Scottish weights and measures would be abolished and replaced by those used in England.

The People and the Union

Daniel Defoe wrote, 'I have never seen a nation where everyone is so angry.' Another English spy reported, 'In Edinburgh and in the North, they complain bitterly against the Union and curse the men who agreed to it. You will meet fifty men against it before you meet one who supports it.'

Defoe added, 'In a corner of a street you can see a Presbyterian minister, a Roman Catholic priest and an Episcopalian vicar all speaking against the Union - but for opposing reasons.'

The Presbyterians were worried that a British Parliament might force the Church of Scotland to have bishops again. They made such a fuss that the government had to pass the 'Act of Security for the Church of Scotland'. This gave the ministers the promises they wanted about never having bishops.

The Jacobites were against the Union because it accepted the Hanoverian Succession. They wanted the son of James VII and II to be king. They were quite prepared to do anything to stop the Union. In Glasgow they even joined a Presbyterian mob protesting against the Union.

Some Glaswegians marched on Edinburgh. They hoped a Highland Jacobite army would join them to fight against the Union.

Nothing happened. People said that the Duke of Hamilton had cancelled the plan at the last minute.

In Dumfries, three hundred Covenanters burned a copy of the Articles of Union as a protest.

There were serious disturbances in Edinburgh. Supporters of the Union were jeered and their horse-drawn coaches were pelted with mud. Opponents were cheered. One night, the mob got completely out of hand and smashed all the windows of the Provost's

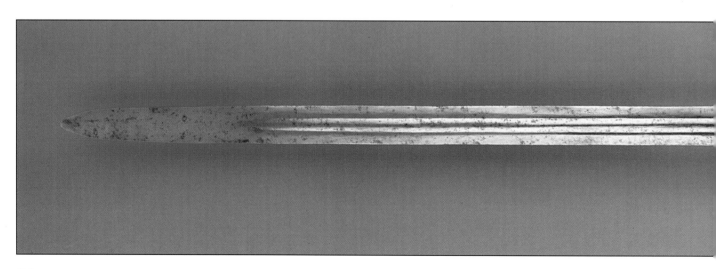

house because he supported the Union. Parliament then banned the mob from the streets and threatened to use the soldiers of the Town Guard against them.

Almost everybody in Scotland was against the Union. That did not matter because the Government made sure that most people in Parliament supported it.

In the Highlands, the Gaelic poet, Iain Lom, heard that the chief of the Clan MacKenzie had been paid a huge amount of money to support the Union.

Iain Lom was furious. In his 'Song Against the Union' he wrote about what he wanted to do to MacKenzie.

He wanted to melt the gold MacKenzie had been given and to pour it into MacKenzie's head so it burned its way right down to his boots!

He also called Hamilton a 'double-dealer' who knew how to sell Scotland.

The Dunfermline Petition

Parliament received many anti-Union petitions. Argyll ignored them all and said that they were only 'fit for making kites.' This petition was from Dunfermline in Fife:

'To Parliament from the Town Council and Inhabitants of Dunfermline.

This plan for a union is against the honour and laws of Scotland. It will destroy the true interests of this nation.

Our ancestors fought to defend these for nearly two thousand years. We want to pass them on to people in the future. We are sure that you will not allow any such union.'

Sir Peter Halket was the Member of Parliament for Dunfermline. He gave this petition to Parliament but then he voted in favour of the Union.

Sir Peter had been given the right to sell his coal to foreigners free from tax.

Words engraved on this Jacobite sword say that its user was against the Union.

The Union in Parliament

The debate in Parliament. Saltoun (left) grew angrier, but Queensberry and Argyll ignored him. They knew they were going to win when Hamilton changed sides.

It is important to remember that some Scots, like the Earl of Cromartie, believed a Union was best for Scotland.

The Earl of Roxburghe said that there were many reasons why people wanted it: 'Trade with most, Hanover with some, security for the others as well as a fear of great poverty and more bad government.'

Roxburghe even talked of '...giving up a name and a poor, independent country for a small share in a great one.'

It soon became clear to everyone that the Duke of Queensberry, who had taken over running the Queen's government from the Duke of Argyll, had the support of most people in Parliament. He ignored the protests and petitions from almost everywhere in Scotland.

Opponents of the Union had to find a different way of stopping him.

First of all, they asked all the Scottish voters to come to Edinburgh. They planned to send a 'National Address' to the Queen asking her to call a General Election. They were sure the voters would elect people who were against the Union.

Their meeting broke up when the Duke of Hamilton started an argument with the Jacobites about the Hanoverian Succession.

Then the opposition planned to protest that the Act of Union was changing Scotland too much but making no changes to England. They planned to demand a General Election.

The Duke of Hamilton was supposed to lead the protest but he stayed away from Parliament because, he said, he had a toothache.

While this was happening, the Duke of Queensberry continued to push the Union through Parliament. Opponents turned up to speak against it. Some of these speeches, like Lord Belhaven's, were printed afterwards to encourage the opposition outside Parliament.

These speeches had no effect.

This is the result of the last vote on the Union:

	For	Against
Nobles	42	19
Shires	38	30
Burghs	30	20
TOTAL	110	69

The Earl of Seafield, who had also worked hard for the Union, commented: 'There's an end to an old song.'

Belhaven's Speech

Here is part of Belhaven's speech to Parliament against the Union:

'When I think about this Union I have some very sad thoughts.

'I see a free and independent kingdom giving up what every nation has fought for: the power to manage its own affairs, by itself and without the help of anyone else.

'I see the noble Lords of Scotland robbed of their followers and a taxman getting more respect than them.

'I see merchants, walking along deserted streets, turned out of their old businesses and wondering what to do next.

'I think I see good tradesmen loaded with new taxes, drinking water instead of ale.

'I see the hardworking farmer unable to sell his grain, cursing the day he was born, and worried about the expense of his funeral.

'I see our ancient mother Scotland, sitting in the middle of our Parliament, waiting for the fatal blow.'

The Earl of Seafield said that Belhaven's speech was written just to 'stir up the common people.'

The Union Today

The Houses of Parliament today.

The Act of Union came into effect on 1 May 1707. There were celebrations in London, but the Act was very unpopular in Scotland.

Supporters of the Union were disappointed by it. There were no immediate benefits for Scotland. The bad effects were seen very quickly. New taxes and tax collectors were very unpopular.

Parliament in London made some changes that annoyed the Scots. It upset the Church of Scotland by giving landowners the right to choose ministers. This was against the Church of Scotland's Presbyterian ideas.

Indeed, by 1713 even the Earl of Seafield, who had worked hard for the Union in the Scottish Parliament, wanted to end it. The Jacobites won support by promising to abolish the Act of Union.

Gradually, Scottish opinion began to change. Some Scots began to think of themselves as 'British'. Many gave up speaking Scots or Gaelic and spoke English instead.

When Britain became richer during the Industrial Revolution and the British Empire grew, many Scots grew proud of being 'British'. They called Glasgow 'the second city of the Empire'.

The Scots, however, have always kept their idea of 'being Scottish'.

In modern times, many Scots have decided they want a separate Scottish Parliament. The Scottish National Party (SNP) want Scotland to become an independent country again. The Labour Party and the Liberal Democrats want a 'Scottish Assembly' to govern Scotland but still to be a part of Britain. This idea is called 'Devolution'. The Conservatives do not want any changes. They say changes would harm the Union and be bad for Scotland.

In 1979 the Scots had a chance to vote for a Scottish Assembly. In a referendum, everyone was given a vote. Thirty-three per cent voted 'Yes' for the Assembly, 31% voted 'No' and 36% did not vote at all. Without at least 40% 'Yes' votes, the referendum rules said that there would be no Scottish Assembly. Many supporters of a Scottish Assembly felt cheated by the 40% rule.

For many people, the idea of Scottish Home Rule has not gone away, but they still have great difficulty in deciding what they want to do about it.

In 1707, Fletcher of Saltoun saw that there was no way for the Scots to change the Act of Union if they became unhappy with it.

He said, 'This will be the result of being one country and not two. It will be turned against the Scots, and the Scottish Members of Parliament can dance around to all Eternity in a trap they made for themselves.'

Such a Parcel of Rogues

Robert Burns, Scotland's most famous poet, worked as a taxman for the British Government. He wrote this poem about the men who voted for the Union.

Fareweel to a' our Scottish fame,
Fareweel our ancient glory!
Fareweel ev'n to the Scottish name,
Sae famed in martial story!
Now Sark rins over Solway sands,
An' Tweed rins to the ocean,
To mark where England's province stands -
Such a parcel of rogues in a nation!

What force or guile could not subdue
Thro' many warlike ages
Is wrought now by a coward few
For hireling traitor's wages.
The English steel we could disdain,
Secure in valour's station;
But, English gold has been our bane -
Such a parcel of rogues in a nation!

O, would that I had seen the day
That treason thus could sell us,
My auld grey head had lien in clay,
Wi Bruce and loyal Wallace!
But, pith and power, till my last hour,
I'll mak this declaration:-
'We're bought and sold for English gold' -
Such a parcel of rogues in a nation!

Glossary

Abolish To get rid of something, like the Committee of the Articles or bishops.

Aragon A region of Spain which was once a country.

Bribe Money paid to a person to buy his or her support. It is against the law.

Burgh The Scots word for town. In England it is spelled 'borough'.

Caledonia The Latin word for Scotland. New Caledonia was the name of the Scottish colony in Darien.

Castile A region of Spain which was once a country.

Civil War When the people in one country go to war with each other.

Colonies Areas of land abroad that a country says belongs to it and where its people have settled.

Committee of the Articles After the Union of the Crowns in 1603, this group of men was selected by the king to do all the work of the Scottish Parliament.

Commonwealth The name that Cromwell gave to the British Republic.

Company A group of people who want to trade.

Company of Scotland The Scottish company that was set up at the end of the seventeenth century to trade with Africa and the Indies. It was ruined by the Darien Disaster.

Covenant A religious word meaning an 'agreement'. Most Scots signed the National Covenant of 1638, which was said to be between the Scots and God and against King Charles I.

Covenanter A Presbyterian who believed in the ideas of the National Covenant, and disagreed with the religious laws of King Charles II so much that he was prepared to fight against the King.

Democracy A system of government in which the people choose who runs the country.

Divine Right of Kings The idea that rulers were special people because God had chosen them to rule. Rulers often used this idea to support their wish to rule by themselves and without any Parliament.

East India Company The name of the company set up in 1600 that had the English monopoly for trade with India.

Episcopalian Protestant Christians whose Church is organized by bishops.

Equivalent The money the Scots were given to make up for them having to pay a share of the English national debt after the Union.

Estates The Scottish Parliament was often called the 'Estates'.

Guardians of Scotland A committee that governed Scotland when there was no ruler for the country.

Hanoverian Succession The law that said that, after Queen Anne died, the throne would go to her Protestant relations in Hanover in Germany.

House of Commons The part of Parliament that is elected by the people.

Jacobite A supporter of King James VII of Scotland and I of England, his son (James Francis, who the Jacobites called James VIII) and grandson (Charles Edward Stuart, who is often called Bonnie Prince Charlie).

Laird The Scots word meaning landowner.

Majority More than half of a group.

Minister A person chosen by the ruler to help govern the country.

Minority Less than half of a group.

Monarch A ruler, usually a king or queen.

Monopoly When only one person or business is allowed to make, buy or sell something.

National debt The money owed by a country or state in payment of the money it has borrowed.

Negotiate Discussing a plan with others until a solution is reached that makes the plan acceptable to all those involved. It usually involves one group offering something if another offers something else in return.

Parliament Members of Parliament (MPs) are elected by the people to make laws and help decide how the country is governed.

Presbyterians Protestants who want the members of the church to control it for themselves.

Privy Council Government ministers and the ruler met in the Privy Council to discuss the running of the country.

Protestants Christians who do not accept the religious ideas taught by the Pope in Rome.

Provost A mayor.

Prussia A country, now part of Germany.

Referendum When everyone is allowed to vote about an important question that affects the whole country.

Reformation When Protestants broke away from the Roman Catholic Church in the sixteenth century.

Roman Catholics Christians who accept the religious ideas taught by the Pope in Rome.

Succession, Law of Rules about who would become the next monarch. Usually this was the eldest male in the family. Parliament had to make a Law of Succession when the Protestant Stuart family died out.

Union Flag (or Union Jack) The flag that combines the flags of Scotland and England. The Irish flag was added after the Irish Act of Union in 1800.

Union of the Crowns After 1603, the ruler of Scotland was also the ruler of England.

Union of Parliaments The Act of Union, 1707, which combined Scotland and England under a single British Parliament.

Further Information

Books to read

The following titles give additional information on some periods of Scottish history mentioned in this book:

Bruce's Scotland by Mari Spankie (Wayland, 1994)

The Highland Clearances by Donald Gunn and Mari Spankie (Wayland, 1993)

The Jacobites by Iain Rose (Wayland, 1995)

Places to visit

Advocates Hall, Edinburgh. This is open to the public only at certain times of the year.

Covenanters' Memorials can be seen in the Grassmarket and Greyfriars Churchyard in Edinburgh. More monuments can be found across South West Scotland where Covenanters were killed.

Edinburgh Castle. The Honours of Scotland are kept here.

Sites of the battles of Montrose, including: Philiphaugh, near Selkirk (prisoners were slaughtered at Newark Castle); Inverlochy, seen from the viewpoint near Inverlochy Castle where many prisoners were slaughtered; Alford, fought on the Gallowhill overlooking Alford; Kilsyth, fought on the outskirts of the modern town.

BBC Education Scotland has produced a range of resources on the Union of 1707.

For TV: *Act of Union* in *Around Scotland* (transmission, Spring 1996).

Software: *1707: The Lost Parliament*, a Hypercard software pack for the Apple Macintosh, developed in co-operation with Strathclyde University, Jordanhill Campus.

Wallchart and Activities Pack: *The Union of 1707*, developed in co-operation with Pictorial Charts Educational Trust. Consultant: Iain Rose.

Information on ordering print and software support material is available from:
BBC Education Scotland, Room 305, 5 Queen Street, Edinburgh EH2 1JF.
Telephone: 0131 469 4262.

Index